DID YOU KNOW ?

FACTS ABOUT THE CONTINENTS

SHEEBA RETIWALLA

Made with ♥ on the Notion Press Platform
www.notionpress.com

For a fresh start

Contents

Foreword

This book is made with a lot of efforts. I really hope you learn something from it.

Acknowledgements

Thankyou Notion Press for this opportunity.

CHAPTER ONE

Asia

1. Singapore is one of only 3 surviving city-states in the world. The other two are Monaco and the Vatican City
2. Thailand has a college just for monkeys. It's called Thani Monkey college and the students learn all sorts of street-performing tricks, as well as how to collect coconuts.
3. The forbidden city, a palace complex in Beijing (China), contains about 9,000 rooms.
4. The largest flower in the world 'Rafflesia' was first discovered by Louis Deschamps in Java (Indonesia). Its bloom can extend more than 3 feet.
5. The world's largest insect is Chan's Megastick which can Measure up to 56.6 cm and be first found in Sabah (Malaysia)
6. Kopi Luwak, The world's most expensive coffee is from Indonesia. It is produced from coffee beans which have been digested by an Indonesian Cat-like animal called the palm civet or civet cat
7. Merlion, Singapore's iconic emblem, is a mythical creature with a lion's head and a fish's tail
8. Hong Kong has the most skyscrapers in the world
9. In China, every year is represented by one of the 12 animals: rat, ox, tiger, rabbit, dragon, snake, horse, goat, monkey, rooster, dog, and pig
10. Thailand is the only Southeast Asian country that has never been colonized the Thai language name of the country is Parthet Thai which means land of the free.
11. 7th-century emperor Tang of Shang of China had 94 icemen who made him ice cream
12. Sultan Salahuddin Abdulaziz Shah roundabout located at Putrajaya in Malaysia is the biggest roundabout in the world it is 3.5 km in diameter
13. Square watermelons are produced in Japan to ease farmers burden to stack and store them
14. Angkor Wat, a temple complex at Angkor (Cambodia) is the world's largest religious building it was built as the state temple and capital for king Suryavarman III

CHAPTER TWO

Africa

1. Ancient Egyptians shaved off their eyebrows to mourn the death of their cat.
2. Europe and Africa are only separated by 14.3 km of ocean and there are talks of creating the longest Bridge ever.
3. Timbuktu, Mali is home to one of the oldest universities in the world established in 1982CE
4. The san people of southern Africa today use the same set of tools that were found in a cave dating to 44,000.
5. A single tribe in Kenya -called " Kalenjin" - produces most of the world's fastest long-distance runners.
6. Africa has the world's largest desert, the Shara, which is almost the size of the United States. It also has the world's tallest and largest land animals, the giraffe, and African elephant, respectively.
7. Almost half the gold ever mined on earth has come from a single place - Witwatersrand, South Africa.
8. South Africa is called the "Rainbow Nation" because it has 11 official languages.
9. The Serengeti (Tanzania) hosts the world's largest wildlife migration on Earth with over 750,000 zebra marching ahead of 1.2 million wildebeest as they cross this amazing landscape.
10. There are more people speaking French in Africa than in France.
11. 2200 years ago, Eratosthenes estimated the circumference of the Earth using math, without ever leaving Egypt, he was surprisingly accurate, and Christopher Columbus later studied him.
12. If you find a meteorite in South Africa, it must be surrendered to the nearest authorities, it's protected under the National Heritage Law.
13. The Ancient Egyptians were the first to make a sweet treat from a marshmallow plant when they combined its sap with nuts and honey.
14. The hippopotamus is Africa's deadliest animal. It kills more people in Africa than do crocodiles and lions combined.

CHAPTER THREE

Europe

1. The world-famous Koh-I - Noor diamond was cut in Amsterdam.
2. The most popular sport in Italy is football. Italy has won four World Cups, in 1934, 1938, 1990, and 2006.
3. The world's greatest cycle race, the Tour de France, has been around for more than 100 years with the first event held on 1 July 1903 Every July, cyclists race some 3,200 km primarily around France in a series of stages over 23 days.
4. The thousand-year-old Bowthorpe Oak in Manthorpe, Lincolnshire, is the largest living oak tree in Britain.
5. The Hermitage Museum in St. Petersburg is home to around 70 cats They guard its treasures against rodents.
6. Norway has won the largest number of Gold, Silver, and Bronze medals of all countries in the Winter Olympics.
7. The first Olympic Games took place in 776 BC The first Olympic champion was a Greek cock named Coruebus who won the sprint race.
8. Norway has the world's deepest underwater tunnel, reaching a depth of 287 meters.
9. There are taxes for owning a dog in Switzerland. These taxes are determined by the dog's size and weight Dog owners are also required to take a training course to learn. how to properly care for their pets.
10. Greek has been spoken for more than 3,000 years, making it one of the oldest languages in Europe.
11. The light bulb, calculator, pocket watch, petrol/Diesel engines, motorcycle, jet engine, LCD screens and the walkman - all invented in Germany.

North America

1. One out of every eight Americans has been employed by McDonald's at some point.
2. On the California-Mexico border, there's a town called Calexico, and on the opposite side, there's a town called Mexicali.
3. Though most Americans speak English, they do not have an official national language.
4. Chicago is the birthplace of the first-ever Ferris wheel, which was 264 feet tall and debuted at the 1893 World's Fair.
5. The tallest mountain in the world is actually located in the United States. It actually taller than Mount Everest. It's called Mount Kea and s located in Hawaii it is only 1796 feet in altitude above sea level when measured from the seafloor it's over 32000 feet high.
6. Also called the Fourth of July US Independence Day marks the historic date in 1776 when the Declaration of Independence was approved by a group called the Continental Congress.
7. Alaska was purchased from Russia in 1867 and is the largest state in the US by land area.
8. Canada has more lakes than the rest of the world's lakes combined.
9. Canada's lowest recorded temparature was - 81.4 degrees Fahrenite (-63 C) in 1942
10. 3 billion pizza's are eaten by Americans annually.

CHAPTER FIVE

South America

1. 92% of all new sold cars in Brazil use ethanol as fuel, which is produced from sugar cane
2. 50 beavers were introduced into Tierra del Fuego, Argentina, in the 1940s to help start a fur trade. There are now over 100,000, and they have devastated over 16 million hectares land.
3. The Atacama desert in Chile is considered the driest place on Earth.
4. The Amazon river carries more water than the world's other 10 biggest rivers combined.
5. The Amazon rainforests are habitat to around half of the world's species of plants and animals. It is also called the Lungs of the Planet', producing 20% of the oxygen on the Earth.
6. With a wingspan of over 10 feet, the Andean Condor is the largest Raptor in the entire world. Fully grown adults can reach a whopping 15 kg and can stand an impressive 12 meters tall.
7. Brazil is home to more than 80 Species of Monkeys this is more species than any other country in the world.
8. The Avenia 9 de Julio in Buenos Aires Argentinal is the widest venue in the world with 12 lanes and is 460 wide.
9. The Catatumbo lightning phenomenon over the mouth of the Catatumbo River where it empties into Lake Maracaibo in Venezuela has been awarded the Guinness World Record for the area with the most lightning.
10. The potato is originally from Peru, and there are over 3,000 different varieties.
11. Forget the Sahara Desert, Peru actually has the highest sand dune in the World Cerro Blanco sand dune, located in the Sechura Desert in the south of Peru, measures 3,860 feet from the baseto the summit.
12. Peru's Nazca Lines, a collection of more than 70 giant human and animal geoglyphs, were first noticed from the air in 1927. They remain one of the world's greatest archaeological mysteries.
13. The Colombian national anthem is played on the radio The stones that were used and television every day at 6AM and 6PM by law.
14. The stones that were used to build Christ the Redeemer statue in Rio de Janeiro (Brazi) came from Sweden.
15. 92% of all new sold cars in Brazil use ethanol as fuel, which is produced from sugar cane
16. 50 beavers were introduced into Tierra del Fuego, Argentina, in the 1940s to help start a fur trade. There are now over 100,000, and they have devastated over 16 million hectares land.
17. The Atacama desert in Chile is considered the driest place on Earth.
18. The Amazon river carries more water than the world's other 10 biggest rivers combined.
19. With a wingspan of over 10 feet, the Andean Condor is the largest Raptor in the entire world. Fully grown adults can reach a whopping 15 kg and can stand an impressive 12 meters tall.
20. Brazil is home to more than 80 Species of Monkeys this is more species than any other country in the world.

Australia

1. More than 85% of Australians live within 50km of the coast.
2. Australia's Highway 1 is the world's longest national highway. With about 14,500 km, (9,000 mi) it circumnavigates the entire country
3. First photos from the moon landing were beamed to the rest of the world from Honeysuckle Tracking Station, near Canberra.
4. Australia was inhabited by indigenous people for about 50,000 years before the British came.
5. If all the sails of the Opera House roof were combined, they would create a perfect sphere. The architect was inspired while eating an orange
6. The world's oldest fossil, which is about 3.4 billion years old, was found in Australia.
7. New Zealand was undiscovered and completely devoid of human beings no more than 800 years ago
8. The dingo fence, which stretches from the Great Australian Bight in SA to central Queensland, is the longest fence in the world (5614km).
9. The Great Barrier Reef, off the coast of Queensland in northeastern Australia, is the largest living structure
10. The male Lyrebird, native to Australia, can mimic the calls of over 20 other birds. He can also imitate the sound of camera, chainsaw and car alarm.
11. Fraser Island, located along the southern coast of Queensland in Australia is the only place in the world where the rainforest grows on sand.
12. The oldest known fossil penguin species lived in the early Paleocene epoch of New Zealand, about 62 million years ago.
13. If you visited one new beach in Australia every day, it would take over 2 years to see them all.

CHAPTER SEVEN

Antarctica

1. The highest temperature ever recorded in Antarctica is 145°C.
2. Australia claims to own the largest territory in Antarctica: 5.8 million sq km (22 million sq mi). Antarctica is almost 1.5 times the size of the US.
3. Antarctica is the largest desert in the world. It is also the coldest, windiest, highest and driest continent on Earth.
4. The largest iceberg ever measured is bigger than 11,000 sq km (4,200 sq mi). It broke away from Antarctica in 2000.
5. Ants have colonized almost every landmass on Earth except for Antarctica and a few remote or inhospitable islands.
6. Antarctica was once covered in rich green forests and inhabited by dinosaurs, during one of Earth's warmest cycles.
7. The ice sheet of Antarctica has been in existence for at least 40 million years.
8. Some parts of Antarctica have had no rain or snow for the last 2 million years.
9. Chile has a civilian town in Antarctica, complete with a school, hospital, hostel, post office, Internet, TV, and mobile phone coverage.
10. 90% of the world's freshwater is in Antarctica.
11. The southernmost active volcano on Earth is Antarctica. It spews crystals and is very close to the US Research Center.
12. There are 300 lakes beneath Antarctica that are kept from freezing by the warmth of Earth's core.
13. Antarctica was once as warm as modern-day California. Now, winds in some places of Antarctica can reach 320 km/h (200 mph).
14. The coldest place on Earth is a high ridge in Antarctica where temperatures can dip below-133°F (-932°C).

This is my first book I will publish more books hoping for a good response.